FOOTBALL SKILLS

PaRragon

Bath • New York • Singapore • Hong Kong • Cologne • Delhi
Melbourne • Amsterdam • Johannesburg • Auckland • Shenzhen

This edition published by Parragon in 2011

Parragon
Queen Street House
4 Queen Street
Bath BA1 1HE, UK

Copyright © Parragon Books Ltd 2011

Photography © PA Photos

All information correct as of January 2011

ISBN 978-1-4454-5243-2

Printed in China

FOOTBALL
SKILLS

CONTENTS

INTRODUCTION

The beautiful game of football is one of the most popular sports in the world. It is packed with drama, speed, power, fantastic skills and tricks, and of course, plenty of spectacular goals. The best teams and players bring enjoyment to millions of fans every season with top stars like Spain's Fernando Torres, England's Wayne Rooney and Argentina's Lionel Messi. These players know that working hard as part of a team is more important than individual effort.

Practice Makes Perfect

Even the most gifted players have to put in hours and hours of practice to perfect their football skills on the pitch. Stars such as Cesc Fàbregas, Kaká and Didier Drogba spend much of their time on the training ground practising even the most basic skills, like shooting, dribbling and passing. With practice comes the accuracy and confidence they need in those crucial match moments.

Footy Skills

This book will take you through all the skills and techniques needed for you to become a star footballer, improving both your confidence and knowledge of the game.

- Techniques are broken down and illustrated with action photography.
- Top tips to help you in training and matches.
- Star player skills show you the strengths of the world's top players in action.

Grab your boots and get practising so you can become a top footballer. Remember: practice makes perfect!

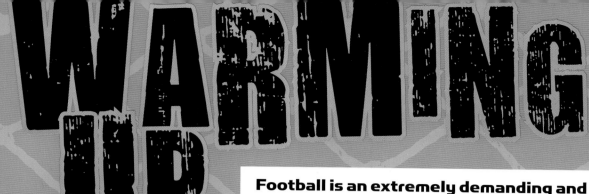

WARMING UP

Football is an extremely demanding and energetic sport as outfield players have to cover many kilometres throughout a game. Players also have to sprint as fast as they can, change direction sharply, and stretch and lunge for the ball in all sorts of directions.

Warming up and stretching your muscles is a big part of pre-match and training preparation. It will help you avoid niggling injuries and enhance your performance right from kick-off and throughout the game.

A good warm-up session can last between 10 and 20 minutes. Players often begin with some very light jogging which may move on to skipping and running gently, but with high knee-lifts to the front and other similar moves added. The main aim is to increase your heart rate so that it is pumping the blood around your body at a good rate and ensuring that all your muscles are ready for movement.

 Remember!

Although running out on the pitch and passing and shooting before a match is fun, don't take the risk. Playing with a cold muscle can cause an injury which may stop you playing as well as you can, or even being able to play at all.

Did you know?

Former Manchester United goalkeeper, Alex Stepney, once dislocated his jaw in a game against Birmingham City in 1975 after shouting at his defenders too much!

Muscle Stretching

After warming up, you are ready to perform a series of stretches to your legs, arms and muscles. Stretches help prepare your muscles for exercise and good stretching helps reduce the risk of injury. A thorough stretching programme will not only cover your legs and feet, but also your back, arms, neck and shoulders.

All stretches should be performed gently and smoothly whilst you ease your body into the stretch. Remember that you should never lunge or bounce into or out of a stretch. For many stretches you can hold a goalpost or use a team-mate to help you balance. Always hold stretches and repeat at least twice so that you complete a full stretching programme.

Top players who rely on their ability to cover distances at great pace need to take extra care to ensure their muscles are fully stretched and ready for action. Speedy strikers like Spain's Fernando Torres and Cameroon's Samuel Eto'o need to make sure their hamstrings – the large muscles at the back of each thigh – are fully warmed up, as they will be tested when the players sprint in short, sharp bursts to get to the ball ahead of their marker.

Did you know?

When playing for former club Athletico Madrid in Spain, Fernando Torres was named club captain at the tender age of 19.

 ## Side-bend Stretch

This side bend will stretch your upper back, arm and stomach muscles. Bend to one side whilst holding your opposite arm overhead, then reverse the direction and bend to the other side. Repeat ten times, always easing into the stretch.

Calf Stretch

The calf muscle is the large muscle on the back of your lower leg. This needs to be stretched well before playing football. One technique shown here is with the front leg bent and the back leg straight with the sole of the foot flat on the floor.

 ## Quadriceps Stretch

The large muscle on the front of your thigh is the quadriceps or 'quad'. One way of stretching it is to hold your foot and, with your body upright, ease it gently back so that your heel reaches your bottom. Hold the position and repeat with both legs.

 ## Groin Stretch

The groin muscles around the pelvis and the inner thigh often bear the brunt of sudden twists or changes of direction during football. There are a number of different stretches for the groin. This method sees you sit on the ground with the soles of your feet together, your knees bent and your back straight. Gently press your knees downward and hold for 10–20 seconds before relaxing. Repeat once more.

Final Preparations

While warming up and stretching isn't the most fun thing in football, it's as vital a part of your performance as keeping your eye on the ball. The warm-up before a game is the perfect time to get fully prepared and ensure you are ready for the challenges ahead. When your muscles are fully stretched, you can take part in some simple drills and exercises designed to get you used to the pitch.

Concentrate on these drills and try your best in each one to make sure that you get the benefit once the game has kicked off. Watch the ball when you hit passes and see how fast or slow the pitch is. These details can make a great difference during the game. Finally, adjust any of your clothing, shin pads, check your boot laces and take a few sips of water.

Looking after your boots and shin pads is really important. Make sure you clean your boots and dry them each time you use them, so that they are ready for the next game. If you feel good in your kit, you will feel more comfortable on the pitch and probably play better.

Did you know?

Some early football boots were made of thick leather that stretched above the ankle. The toe area was made of hardened leather and it was usual for players to toe-punt the ball rather than use the instep.

Control

A few runs through a slalom of cones allows you to practise your dribbling and close control of the football shortly before a match.

BALL CONTROL

Practising ball control, cushioning and shielding is a vital part of helping you play your best on the pitch. Some of the most naturally talented players from all over the world have honed their skills after hours and hours of practice with just a ball for company. Good control can often gain you extra time and space, two things that are extremely precious in football.

Only sometimes will the ball travel to you at the ideal height, speed and angle. Football is such a dynamic game that the ball bounces and deflects off players and the ground at different angles. Learning to control the ball accurately and quickly, however it reaches you, will help you to turn the most difficult of passes, crosses and throws into controlled possession for your team.

Cushion Expert: Thierry Henry

A former World Cup and European Championship winner with France, Thierry Henry scored many of his goals after brilliant thigh and chest control which allowed him to get the ball down quickly, before using his pace to drift around defenders and create space for a shot at goal.

First Touch

Your first touch of the ball is crucial. Next time you're watching your favourite players, concentrate on their first touch when the ball comes to them. The quality of a player's first touch will influence whether they need to take a second or third touch to get the ball under control. The longer you take to get the ball under your spell, the harder it will be to play the best pass or shot as opposition players will be putting you under pressure.

Firm Control

Most of the time you will want to cushion the ball in order to kill its speed and quickly get it under control at your feet. In some situations, though, you can use much firmer control to make a short, effective pass to a team-mate, or to push the ball into space ahead of you to run on to. Getting in line with the ball is still important, but as it arrives, instead of relaxing and moving the part of your body that will strike the ball back, you should keep it firm and, if you want extra distance, thrust forward to push the ball away and down.

Sidefoot Cushion

You can control the ball instantly with the side of your foot, taking the pace out of a firm pass and keeping it the perfect distance in front of you in preparation for your next touch. To perform the sidefoot cushion, line yourself up with the ball as it comes toward you, lifting your leg and turning your ankle so that the side of your foot is facing the ball. Then, keep your foot as still as possible and either allow the ball to roll onto it, or move it slightly towards the ball to meet its movement.

12

Sidefoot

The inside length of your foot is known as your sidefoot. The inside arch of your foot makes a broad area which contacts the ball. As a result, it is thought of as the most accurate method to strike the ball and the most commonly used technique in passing. It can also be used for short-range shots on goal. Many strikers like to use this technique to 'pass' the ball into the net.

The sidefoot push-pass is the most frequently used pass in a football match. You will see it utilized by defenders as they play the ball to other members of the defence. You will also see it used in rapid, one-touch passing plays in midfield and attack as one team tries to pass the ball around to create space and the chance to take a shot at goal. The sidefoot is best used over shorter distances where you are aiming to send the ball zipping across the surface of the pitch.

Sidefoot Expert: Pelé

To be honest, as arguably the best footballer of all time, Brazilian star Pelé could be an expert for every single skill, but his ability to control and pass the ball with his sidefoot, showing great speed and accuracy, helped create countless scoring opportunities for himself and his team-mates. Pelé was capable of dribbling and beating men with skill, but his vision and decision-making with his passes were fantastically effective.

Place your standing foot to the side of the ball and get your body over the ball as you swing your kicking foot back. Try to keep your head up to check out the game ahead of you.

Shielding

A lot of the time when you receive the ball, your opponents won't be too far away from you. They will be looking to close you down, put pressure on your touch and intercept the ball. In these situations, you will need to get the ball under control and use your body as a shield, placing it between the ball and your opponent so that they cannot make an easy challenge for the ball or knock you off balance.

You cannot just stand there, nor can you push the opponent away or tug at his shirt, otherwise the referee is likely to award a free kick to the other team. The same thing will probably happen if you try to block or obstruct an opponent by standing in front of the ball. It's important to remember that the ball must be under your control as you shield it.

1. As the ball arrives, this player senses an opponent coming to close him down. He turns to get his body between the defender and the ball.

2. Stay aware of where your opponent is and keep moving with the ball under control.

3. Without pushing your opponent, try to make yourself as big as possible to block them.

STRIKING

There are many different ways you can move the ball around the pitch with your feet. Different parts of your foot and different techniques can send the ball a short distance or most of the length of the pitch, depending on what's required. You can hit the ball with great speed and real venom or use much less pace and force to make a delicate pass.

The best way to strike a ball can change from second to second during a match. For example, you may consider a full strike of the ball using the instep drive, then at the last moment change your mind to play a short pass to a team-mate. The more skilled you are with a range of different striking techniques, the more choice you will give yourself in a match and the harder it will be for defenders to mark you, as they won't know what you are going to do next.

Fun drills and games will help build your confidence and skill at striking the ball under pressure. Get together with two other players and practise quick, accurate short passes, keeping the ball in an area marked out by cones. One player can try to intercept the ball or force a mistake from the defenders.

Instep Drive

Your instep is where the boot laces run across the top of your foot. It is a good-sized, largely flat area which allows for powerful, long-distance passes or strikes on goal. It can generate a lot more force than the sidefoot pass.

The regular instep drive sees you get your body weight over the ball to help keep the ball's flight down. If you want to send the ball higher, for example, to send a long high clearance downfield or to make a cross from the sideline into the area for a header, you can use a lofted instep drive. Here, you lean back a little and aim to strike the bottom half of the ball to send it up and forward.

1. To make a good instep drive, plant your non-kicking foot to the side of the ball as your kicking leg swings back. You can stick your arms out to help improve your balance.

2. With your body over the ball, swing your leg forward with the toes pointing downwards so that your boot laces connect with the middle of the ball.

3. Drive your foot through the ball with the ankle stretched out and down. The foot carries on swinging on a long follow-through after the ball has left.

Bending

Most of the time you will want to strike the ball so that it travels in a straight direction, either passing it to a team-mate or shooting into the back of the net. But in some situations you will attempt to bend the ball, sending it on a curving, curling path.

These include taking a corner so that it swings in towards or away from the goal, or bending the ball around the edge of a free-kick wall and towards goal. You can bend the ball with either the inside or outside of your foot. In both cases, you strike the back and one side of the ball. With your foot kicking across the ball and carrying on a long follow-through, you add sidespin to it, which makes it first curve outwards and then inwards. Judging the amount of bend or swerve on the ball is not easy, though, and only comes with experience and lots and lots of practice.

You can bend the ball using the inside of your right boot. Get your standing foot a little way from the ball to give you room to swing your leg. Use the inside of your boot around the toes and left side of the instep to connect with the right-hand side of the ball. Your follow-through takes your foot across your body.

For an outside bend with your right foot, strike the back and left side of the ball with the outside of the top part of your boot, with your toes pointing downwards. Your leg should swing across your body on its long follow-through.

17

Volleys

A volley is when you strike the ball in mid-air. Volleys require excellent technique and timing as the ball is constantly on the move. You have to watch the ball carefully throughout its path as it comes towards you. Even famous footballers who take their eye off the ball or get their timing wrong see their volley attempts end in embarrassment as they miss the ball completely, or thump it high and wide.

Volleys are used in a range of different situations. They can be the quickest way to connect with the ball when it is in the air and flying straight towards you. They can also be used for a first-time strike on goal or a defensive clearance when the ball flies in from a cross. When connecting fully in mid-air with an instep drive, a volley can be the most powerful of strikes, sending the ball screaming towards goal. Controlling the power and placement of a volley requires plenty of practice.

Front On

1. For a front-on volley using your instep, watch the ball carefully as it flies towards you. Keep your head still. Plant your non-kicking foot and lift your kicking leg, leading with your knee which is held high.

2. Point your foot downward as you bring it forward and aim to strike the centre or top half of the ball with your boot instep. Try not to stretch for the ball if you can help it and follow through in the direction of the target.

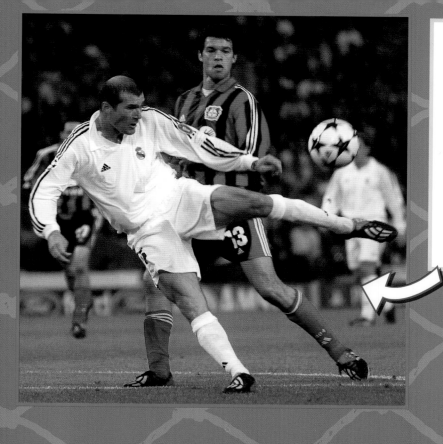

Volley Expert: Zinedine Zidane

The former France captain scored many memorable goals throughout his glorious career, but one that will stand out for many is a spectacular volley in the 2002 European Cup Final against Bayer Leverkusen (left). With the ball dropping out of the air at speed, Zidane flashed a powerful left-footed volley right into the top corner of the goal. His sublime technique, great balance, timing and follow-through helped 'Zizou' score many outstanding volleys.

Did you know?

When making front-on volleys, try to keep your head over the ball as much as possible to help keep it down after you've struck it. You can also stick out your arms to help you balance as you perform a volley.

 ## Side Volley

To make a side volley with the ball around waist height, first get well balanced on your standing foot. Lift your kicking leg at the hip and swing it up and around so that it is parallel or almost parallel to the ground as you connect with the ball. Make sure your foot is over the ball to keep the ball down and strike it with your boot laces.

19

Chipping

A chip is used to get the ball high into the air in a short amount of time and space. It is sometimes used to dink the ball over a defender when there is a large area of space behind the opponent for a team-mate to run into. Most chips, though, are shots on goal, played against a goalkeeper who is some way off their goal line.

The short backswing and stabbing-down movement of your foot sends the ball rising sharply into the air, over the goalkeeper's outstretched arms, then landing sharply, often with some backspin behind the keeper, or straight into the net.

To make a good chip, approach the ball straight on. Place your standing foot beside the ball, not behind it – a common mistake. With your foot angled downwards, aim to strike the bottom of the ball with your instep. Your boot should connect with the ball and the ground at the same time. There is next-to-no follow-through with a good chip.

Chipping Experts: Wayne Rooney

One of England's most talented players, Wayne Rooney has the ability and vision to score chipped goals from both inside and outside the area. Rooney often spots the goalkeeper off his line and chips the ball with great power and dip over the keeper, sending the ball into the back of the net. He uses a short, sharp stabbing motion of his boot to perform this type of effort.

David Beckham

David Beckham is known as one of the best, if not the best, player of the chipped ball. Beckham has proved his ability to chip the ball into goal on countless occasions. One particular example that displays his unbeatable chipping skill was the infamous halfway line goal against Wimbledon in the 1996/7 season. Another impressive chip came in his last goal for Manchester United, against Everton. A free kick combined with an accurate chip over a wall of defenders was all he needed to land the ball in the centre of the net. These goals have undoubtedly gone down in history.

Flicks & Backheels

You can use a flick of your boot to make a short pass to either your left or your right. This underrated skill can be extremely useful when you have received the ball and are under great pressure from a defender stood right behind you.

Attackers often use a backheel when confronted with one or more defenders ahead of them, to move the ball back suddenly to a team-mate behind. Strikers like Thierry Henry, Andrey Arshavin and Robinho have all found themselves with their back to goal, close to the goal line, and used a backheel to surprise the defence and score.

 ## Backheels & Rolls

The back of your boot – the heel area – is curved and doesn't offer a large space to strike the ball. As a result, it tends not to be that accurate, but can be handy when moving the ball over short distances to reverse the direction of play. A quick flick of your boot can play the ball several metres to a team-mate. With your foot to the side of the ball, twist your ankle away from the ball and then flick it back, connecting with the middle of the ball. You can use the inside of your boot or the outside to make contact.

Strike through the middle of the ball with your heel. Don't stab at the ball. Instead, try to keep your foot parallel with the ground and aim for a short but smooth push through the ball.

PASSING

Good, accurate passing can get your team out of danger, move the ball quickly around the pitch quicker than if you were running with it, and lead to goalscoring chances more frequently than any other skill. Players capable of passing the ball consistently well, like Spain's Cesc Fàbregas and Kaká of Brazil, are thought of as playmakers, capable of directing how their team plays.

As the passer, you not only have to get your striking technique right, but you have to hit the ball in a way that reaches your receiver at the ideal pace, height and place for them to control it easily. Your receiver may be sprinting forward into lots of space, in which case you will want to play the ball ahead of them so that they can run on to it, but not so far ahead that they cannot reach it.

This player has made a good sidefoot pass to send the ball a little ahead of his team-mate to run on to. Sidefoot passes are often the most accurate.

23

Passing Expert: Cesc Fàbregas

Arsenal's Cesc Fàbregas is excellent at making quick and accurate passes. He's known as a true pass master! Fàbregas's smooth playing makes it appear he has more time and space on the pitch than anyone else, proving how effective his passing is. Since leaving Spain in 2003, his career has taken off at club level since signing with Arsenal at just 16 years old. At Euro 2008, Fàbregas scored the winning penalty in the Quarter-final shoot-out against Italy, and played an important role in the Final to earn Spain their first major title since 1964. Fàbregas was also involved in the winning goal in the 2010 World Cup, setting up Andres Iniesta's extra-time goal as Spain beat the Netherlands in the Final. Fàbregas's pinpoint passes and angled flicks are always well placed and never fail to impress.

Passing

Striking the ball with the right amount of force or weight is a very important part of passing. Too little weight can lead to the ball falling short or being easily intercepted. Too much and the ball could race off the pitch or be difficult for your team-mate to control.

Disguising Passes

Once your passing game is solid, you can add extra elements such as learning to disguise the pass you intend to make. Top players become skilled at faking to pass in one direction, only to swivel their bodies and feet to make a pass in another direction to a team-mate behind.

The player in red has tricked the defender into thinking he was passing to his right. As the defender moves to try to block the pass, he quickly swivels his foot round and plays the ball the opposite way.

Passing Moves

Teams rehearse simple passing moves such as the one-two pass, which enable them to use one or two passes to make easy progress up the pitch or to get in behind defenders. A through-ball is a pass behind the other team's defence.

They can be deadly, as the defender has to turn to follow the ball and may not recover for a handful of seconds by which time the ball could be in the back of the net, courtesy of a quick-thinking and moving striker. Performing an accurate through-ball requires great timing and weighting of the ball. Keep an eye on the movement of your team-mates and the space ahead of you, pick where you want to play the pass and then concentrate on making the right connection.

Used to play the ball round an opponent to cut them out of the game, a one-two pass is one of the simplest, most common and effective passing moves in football. The first player passes the ball and immediately sprints past the opponent. The receiver, often with their first touch, passes the ball behind the opponent back to their team-mate.

Did you know?

If you cannot see a good attacking pass forward, consider a pass to the side or behind. Changing the angle of attack may lead to a goalscoring chance for your team just a few passes later.

Awareness

If you learn to play with your head up, scanning the game and players around you as much as possible, it will give you a head start in picking out who to pass the ball to. The game changes continually so it's important to focus on everything that's going on around you, and not just look down at the ball trying to dribble past everybody.

Keep an eye out for overlaps where a team-mate looks to make a run down the sideline and past the defence. Also, look out for overloads when more than one player from your team is occupying a similar position and you have a numbers advantage over your opponents.

As soon as you have passed the ball, get moving yourself. Look to get into a position to receive a pass back or to pull a defender out of position. This can create space for another player from your team to move into by running with the ball.

27

SHOOTING

If you don't try to shoot and don't get the ball on target, then you cannot win the game – it's as simple as that. Shooting chances are most likely to come to a team's strikers, but Frank Lampard's 20 goals in the 2009/10 Premier League season show that midfielders often get the chance to shoot.

This is usually either from set pieces or from latching onto the ball around the edge of the penalty area. The ball will also sometimes fall to a defender who has come forward to attack a corner or free kick, so all players should practise their shooting skills.

This midfielder has pounced on a poor defensive pass and hits a shot straight away with the first touch of the ball. Opponents will try to close you down quickly, so don't hesitate if a chance comes your way – act fast.

Shooting Experts: Fernando Torres

Fernando Torres is well known for his goalscoring record. He scored 75 goals in 174 La Liga appearances for Real Madrid. In his debut season for Liverpool in 2007, he scored more than 20 league goals, making him the first player since Robbie Fowler to do so. In the 2007/08 season, he scored 29 goals, beating Michael Owen's record for goals in a season. Torres made his debut for Spain against Portugal and played in the 2010 World Cup squad.

David Villa

David Villa has a fantastic goalscoring ability, scoring from impressive bicycle kicks and lobs from the halfway line. His record speaks for itself – he has hit over a hundred goals for his team, Valencia, and has scored a phenomenal 33 goals in 52 games for Spain. Villa was also top scorer at Euro 2008, with four goals. He is extremely quick on his feet and has all the attacking qualities needed for a star footballer.

Taking Chances

Top goalscorers anticipate where the ball will fall and try to get into position as early as possible to make a shot. They anticipate where the ball may head, so they don't stray offside but get to the ball first, ahead of opponents.

They have just fractions of a second to weigh up the situation and decide what to do. This is why players try to play with their heads up, scanning the game as much as possible. If they are close to the goal line or the ball's path to goal appears blocked by defenders, they may look for a team-mate in a better attacking position than themselves. But mostly, their thoughts are on fashioning an opening to get their own shot away.

Goal-poaching Expert: Carlos Tevez

Carlos Tevez is a footballing dynamo – he is extremely skilled with impressive body language. Of all his extravagant skills, Tevez is at his best supplying poached goals in crowded penalty areas. If tackled, he'll be on his feet again in no time at all! In 2007, Tevez took West Ham to Premiership survival, scoring the only goal in a last-game-of-the-season clincher against Manchester United. With his explosive style and tight control, he is also a hero in South America, with Diego Maradona labelling him the 'Argentine prophet for the 21st century'.

Keeping Confidence

No player's shooting is ever 100% accurate or always leads to goals. Even top strikers like Didier Drogba, Fernando Torres and Wayne Rooney regularly miss good chances to score. A strong mental attitude sees players of this calibre put the mistake out of their mind and get on with the game.

Power & Placement

Only you can decide what type of shot to make in any given situation. If close in on goal, players often opt to use a sidefoot pass to steer the ball into the net away from the goalkeeper. From further out, players may choose to power the ball home with a strong instep drive.

When the ball flies across the six-yard area, it is important to just get any part of your body (but not your hands and arms) on the ball to direct it goalwards. Be brave and don't be afraid to head the ball even if you are surrounded by other players. You have to be in the mix to stand any chance of scoring.

Where you aim the ball will be crucial to scoring success. Keeping the ball low and aiming into the corner furthest from the goalkeeper often leads to success.

31

Use Both Feet

Being able to shoot well with both feet is a major advantage. It means that a defender cannot force you onto your much weaker foot for a shot. It also means that they are unsure which side you will move in order to fire off an effort. In this situation, you have a much greater chance of faking a move to one side before moving to the other to take a strike at goal.

Following Up

Don't admire your shot as it heads towards goal. Get back into the game and follow up your strike or any efforts by your team-mates. Deflections off the goalposts or crossbars, defenders' blocks and goalkeeper's saves often see the ball cannon back into play, giving you a second chance to score.

Did you know?

Trevor Brooking once played a whole game with his weaker left foot when he was a youngster. The former West Ham United and England striker put the work in at an early age to be strong with both feet.

DRIBBLING

Dribbling is all about keeping close control of the football using a series of small nudges and taps of the ball with your feet. It sounds straightforward, and when moving straight ahead into lots of space with no opponents nearby, it often is. But dribbling is used frequently in pressure situations by an attacker trying to get past one or more opponents in order to shoot or make a pass that will lead to a goal.

You can practise dribbling in a small space almost anywhere. Beginners start by getting a feel for the ball at their feet and learn moves at walking pace before gradually building up speed. For dribbling to be successful in a real game, it mostly has to be performed at high speed or with sudden changes of pace and direction.

Dribbling through a line of cones using the inside and outside of your boot is a classic way to practise dribbling in training.

This can be turned into a more competitive exercise by setting out two equal-length cone slaloms and splitting players into two relay teams, with each player having to dribble in and out of the cones without missing any out.

33

Dribbling Expert: Lionel Messi

Lionel Messi is among some of the best players who are keeping the art of dribbling alive. His skills on the ball are astonishing and he can glide past defenders effortlessly, making it impossible for them to react quickly enough. This has made Messi one of the most exciting players of his generation. His speed on the ball, power, incredible balance and strength have even drawn comparisons to Diego Maradona.

Did you know?

Lionel Messi's goal in a 2007 Spanish Cup Semi-final against Getafe was directly compared to Maradona's 'Goal of the Century' against England in the 1986 World Cup.

Taking Risks

There is always a chance that you will lose the ball when dribbling either through your own poor control or a good, accurate challenge by an opponent. This makes dribbling a high-risk tactic and one best carried out in the other team's half.

Try not to dribble the ball when in your own defensive third of the pitch, especially in your penalty area. One small lapse of control and an opponent could take the ball away from you and score. However, it's also important for defenders to work on their close control so they can command the ball in pressurized situations.

Risk Expert: Ashley Cole

The England and Chelsea defender has the natural ability to dribble past opponents and beat them with skill, and knows exactly when to make an accurate cross. Cole can control the ball at speed, put in one well-timed tackle after another, and has great positioning on the pitch at all times.

You should never be afraid to have possession of the ball. Practising your control and ball skills will make you more confident in your own ability when you step onto the pitch.

Committing Defence

Transporting the ball using both feet and changing speed and direction can often lead to successful dribbles, but there are other ways to try to trick a defender and make them commit to move or lunge in one direction, allowing you to get past them by moving in another direction.

You can use exaggerated body movements to pretend or feint as if you intend dribbling in one direction only to move in another, or you can pretend that you are about to shoot or pass, but instead quickly continue to dribble. In all cases, try to make your trick movements as convincing as possible.

 ## Nutmeg

This defender has a very wide stance and the attacker has noted it. He cheekily passes the ball through the defender's legs and races round his opponent to collect the ball on the other side. This is known as a nutmeg. There must be plenty of space behind the defender and your weight of pass must be spot on for this move to work.

Stepover & Dragback

As you develop your dribbling abilities, you might want to add one or two signature moves just like the pros use. Perfect these in training and practise by yourself and with a few friends. You've got to be able to perform these moves quickly and accurately before unveiling them in a proper match.

One popular trick is the dragback, whilst a common feinting move is the stepover. This was popularized by Pelé before becoming fashionable again in recent years by players including Arjen Robben, Joe Cole, Franck Ribéry and, of course, the twinkled-toed Cristiano Ronaldo.

Stepover

Whilst dribbling, plant one foot to the side of the ball and make an exaggerated swing of your other foot around the front of the ball to the other side. If the defender commits to covering what looks like your intended direction, push the ball in the opposite direction and swerve past them.

Dragback

To perform a dragback, start by shaping to play the ball in the direction you are heading. Then, stop the ball with the sole of your boot. Use the sole to drag the ball backwards as you pivot on your other foot, turning to face a different direction before sprinting away.

37

HEADING

Heading is not just for central defenders or strikers. It's a skill required by every player as the ball spends a lot of time in the air in all areas of the pitch.

Learning how to control the height, force and direction of your headers is crucial. Sometimes, a gently cushioned header to one side will turn a difficult bouncing ball into easy possession for your team. Other times, you will want to use plenty of force to power a header upfield or into the back of the opponent's goal.

This player spots a cross coming in and moves towards the ball. They time their jump to get their head a little above the ball. They aim for their forehead to make contact with the ball just above its middle and keep their neck muscles firm to help direct the ball downwards.

Whatever the type of header required, it is tempting to close your eyes and brace yourself for impact. Yet, the most important thing with all types of headers is to watch the ball right onto your head. Try to keep your eyes open as long as you can when heading the ball.

Cushioned Headers

The cushioned header is a great way to control a high ball, either to bring it down in front of your feet or to gently pass it under control to a team-mate. Unlike other headers, you must keep the muscles of your neck and upper body nice and relaxed as you meet the ball.

Flick Ons

This is a valuable skill used mainly in set pieces like wide free kicks and corners. A player uses a sudden backward twist of their neck and head to flick the ball up and past a defender behind them. The aim is to move the ball on to a team-mate behind who may get a chance to score.

Headed Goals

Around one in five of all goals scored come from headers. The good news is that you don't have to be a giant like Peter Crouch or Mario Gomez to score frequently with headers.

Wayne Rooney was not originally known as a great header of the ball, but has worked incredibly hard on his heading and scored an incredible eight headed goals in a row in 2010.

The most important tip to remember about scoring from headers is direction. If possible, try to get your head over the ball so that you can aim it downwards towards the goal and away from the goalkeeper. This often means that you will need to make a powerful spring upwards.

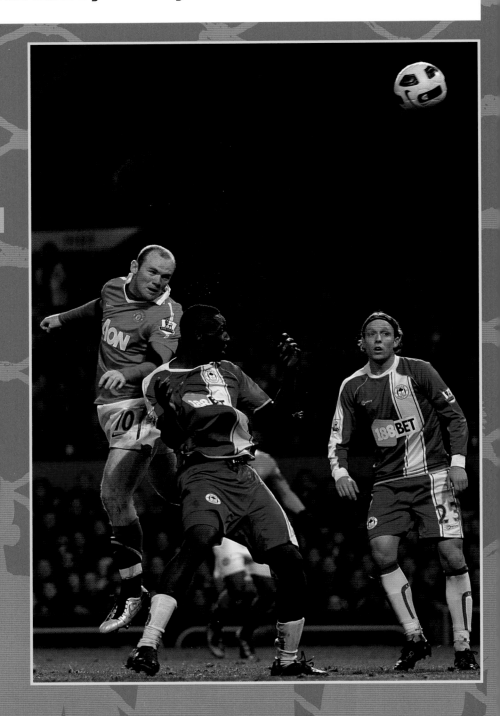

Did you know?

Lionel Messi took Barcelona to Champions League glory with a superb header in 2009, despite being shorter than the average football player.

Clearing Headers

All outfield players will sometimes need to head the ball out of danger, away from their goal from a corner or sending the ball a long distance upfield from the edge of their penalty area.

Time your spring upwards so you meet the ball at or near the top of your jump. Watch the ball and arch your back as you rise in the air.

Keep your neck muscles firm as you thrust your arms back to drive your upper body and head forward to meet the ball. Aim to connect just below the middle of the ball to send it both forwards and upwards to clear it well out of danger.

Heading Expert: Nemanja Vidic

The Serbian international defender is one of the finest in Europe. Vidic uses his great strength and determination to position his body ahead of the attacker before jumping and powering the ball away with great power. He always gets good height and distance on his clearing headers, using the strength of his leg muscles and excellent reading of the game and the flight of the ball.

Defending

Defensive systems and tactics can get complex and detailed, but always remember defence is about two main things: stopping your opponents from scoring, and getting the ball back in your team's possession. As soon as the ball is lost, your team are defending. Players should rush back into position goalside of the ball, meaning they put themselves between the opponent with the ball and their own goal.

The whole team has a part to play in defence, and strikers should chase down and put pressure on opposing defenders and midfielders to deny them time and space to pick their pass. It is surprising that, even at the top level, a quick series of sprints by a defending team's forwards can cause a defender or a goalkeeper in possession of the ball to make a mistake, fluffing their control, dribble or pass.

Through good, hard running by the striker in white, the player on the ball has been forced to make a pass back to his goalkeeper. The goalkeeper may hit the ball long upfield, meaning that it is 50-50 which team will gain possession of the ball.

Marking

Attacking footballers need time and space in which to develop their team's play. They especially need this when receiving the ball and when trying to get into a position close enough to goal to fire off a shot. Marking is a key defensive ploy and helps teams to deny their opponents the time and space to attack.

There are two systems commonly used – zonal marking and one-on-one marking. Zonal marking sees defenders and midfielders guard an area of the pitch. Each of these areas overlaps others to, in theory, provide a complete defence of the final third of the pitch. One-on-one (also known as man-to-man) marking sees individual players guard a single opponent and move with them as they move, stopping them gaining the time and space to receive the ball, turn and head towards goal. Both of these systems can be used when a team is defending a set piece, like a corner or a free kick.

Opponents may try a number of tricks to fool you into making a marking mistake. To get around this, always keep your eye on the ball.

Jockeying

Jockeying is a crucial defensive technique which delays an opponent with the ball. Performed well, it will often buy your team precious seconds to get back into a strong defensive position.

It's important to stay on your feet for as long as possible when trying to tackle your opponent. Do not slide in or go onto the ground unless it's absolutely necessary. Some of the finest defenders rarely get their shorts dirty as they tackle and intercept with both feet firmly on the ground.

From around one or two metres away, the player in blue has cut down his opponent's options in attack. She now has to get past him or pass back or to the side. Staying springy on the balls of his feet, the defender is ready to retreat in a zig-zagging pattern as his opponent moves forward, or dart to one side if they change direction.

44

Tackling

The perfect tackle is one which is both fair and sees the defender win the ball under control for their team. In many situations, you may not be able to gain the ball yourself, but getting the ball away from an opponent's feet and out of their control is still important for your team's defence.

Always try to make a tackle only after you know you have defensive cover behind you. Try to stay on your feet and once committed to make a tackle, don't shy away. There may be some contact between your legs and bodies, but as long as you have timed your movement into the tackle well, it should not hurt.

Block Tackles

Time your approach with your body facing your opponent and then quickly plant your supporting leg, flexed at the knee, before you strike the middle of the ball with the inside of your tackling foot. Timing is crucial, but performed firmly with your entire body weight over the ball, you should dislodge the ball from your opponent.

SET PIECES

Set pieces are ways of restarting the game after the ball has left the pitch, or after a referee has stopped the game for a foul or another rule infringement such as offside. Common set pieces are throw-ins, corners, free kicks and penalties. Many set pieces will be taken in your own half of the pitch. The aim with these is to play the ball so that a team-mate can control it easily and your team is able to keep possession.

When a set piece is in the opponent's half, such as a corner or a free kick, it becomes an attacking set piece where your team can create a goalscoring chance, either by whipping in a cross or deep ball to a team-mate or shooting directly at goal.

A large number of goals are scored from free kicks, corners and penalties. Never waste an opportunity during a set piece. Instead, communicate with team-mates, focus and look to deliver an accurate ball that can lead to a goalscoring chance.

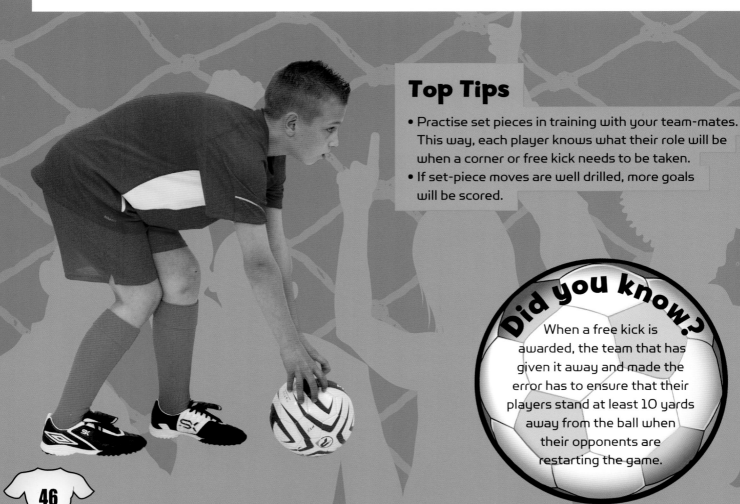

Top Tips

- Practise set pieces in training with your team-mates. This way, each player knows what their role will be when a corner or free kick needs to be taken.
- If set-piece moves are well drilled, more goals will be scored.

Did you know?

When a free kick is awarded, the team that has given it away and made the error has to ensure that their players stand at least 10 yards away from the ball when their opponents are restarting the game.

Throw-Ins

When the ball goes out over the sideline, the game is restarted with a throw-in. Whilst a throw-in is rarely as much of a threat as a corner or an advanced attacking free kick, don't make the mistake of not concentrating fully when your side receive one.

Make sure you follow the rules when taking a throw-in. Even top professional players get penalized for making foul throws, leading to the opposition being awarded a throw-in from the same place. As soon as you have made the throw, get back onto the pitch and in the game. You may be called on immediately to make a run or to receive the ball straight back from the throw.

Top Tips

- Before the ball is thrown forward, it must be taken back behind the head.
- Hands must remain on the ball throughout the throw.

Did you know?

A throw-in is classed as a 'foul throw' for several reasons. It can be if the thrower's feet are over the sideline, the ball isn't thrown over the head or it doesn't actually enter the field of play. Throw-ins cannot be taken one-handed and cannot be taken underarm.

Corners

When taking a corner, be certain what sort of corner you are going to take. A short corner is one hit a short distance to a team-mate nearby. These can catch out defending teams whose players are crowded in the penalty area.

A regular corner is hit with an instep drive pass deep into the penalty area around the front of the six-yard box. This is the danger area where goalkeepers are uncertain whether to come and catch the ball easily or whether they should stay on their line and let their defenders deal with it.

The corner-taker has the choice of sending it towards the near post where a flick-on header from a team-mate can cause havoc, or deep to the back post to coincide with a team-mate making a run into the area.

Whatever type of corner you take, try to hit the ball high enough to beat the first defender, but with plenty of pace. This sees the ball fly fast into the penalty area, without looping up and coming down slowly.

A powerful and quickly struck corner is the hardest to defend against, as any slight deflection could send it flying into the net.

Players skilled at taking corners can perform two types of 'swinging corner'. One is an 'inswinging corner', where a player can put bend on the ball so that it curves towards the goal. The other is an 'outswinging corner', where a player curves the ball away from the goalkeeper and defenders.

Free Kicks

Free kicks are awarded for fouls or offences, such as offsides. If you are close to where the free kick was awarded, you can always consider taking a quick free kick to get play moving whilst opponents are out of position. But make sure your head is up as you go to take the free kick and that the player you intend hitting the ball to is expecting it; otherwise you run the risk of the ball being intercepted.

Defending teams usually treat free kicks with respect. They usually put up a wall of two, three or more players in a line between the free kick and their goal. Getting past the wall is the first priority of the free-kick taker. One way of beating a defensive wall is for one player to shape to shoot, but actually roll the ball to a team-mate who is at an angle to shoot without the wall blocking their attempt.

Take a tip from top free-kick takers like Frank Lampard, Kaká and Mikel Arteta, who are skilled at bending the ball round the edge of the wall or looping it up and over towards goal.

Free-kick Expert: Juninho Pernambucano

Brazilian Juninho is currently one of the best free-kick takers in football. His technique, called 'knuckle balling', involves putting a spinning motion on the ball, causing it to swerve unpredictably and making it hard for the goalkeeper to save. Since May 2009, Juninho has scored 44 goals from direct free kicks during his career for Lyon. On four occasions, he has scored from free kicks beyond 40 metres, his latest success being a 40-metre strike against Marseille in 2009. Juninho has also been hailed as one of the greatest dead-ball specialists of all time. No one else has yet been able to match his technique and consistency of free-kick success.

Did you know?

David Beckham is also hailed as one of the best free-kick takers ever, scoring regularly from free kicks when playing for Manchester United, England and Real Madrid. He is also only the fifth player to score twice from a free kick in a World Cup, against Ecuador and Colombia.

Penalties

A referee awards a penalty for a major foul or offence, such as a deliberate handball by the defending team inside their own penalty area. If you step up to take one, always remember that a penalty provides a superb chance to score.

The ball is placed just 11 metres from the goal with only the goalkeeper to beat and no interference from defenders. Goalkeepers can now move along their goal line before the kick is struck, and in many matches tend to move one or two paces off their line.

Place the ball carefully on the penalty spot and look up to gain a strong mental picture of the goal. Focus on the large areas of net. Decide where you want to place the penalty in advance and don't change your mind during your run-up.

Did you know?

The first ever penalty shoot-out to be held in a professional match in England took place in 1970 between Hull City and Manchester United, and was won by Manchester United.

Stay alert after you have struck the ball. The goalkeeper may parry the ball or it may bounce off the post or crossbar and stay in play. A large number of 'saved' or failed penalties are scored seconds afterwards by a follow-up.

There is no foolproof way of scoring a penalty. Many players prefer to guide the ball low, using a strong sidefoot pass to place the ball low into the corner of the goal. Others gamble on the goalkeeper diving a certain way and so blast the ball using a powerful instep drive straight down the middle.

Whatever you choose, try to avoid hitting the ball so that it travels goalwards at around thigh or waist height, as a goalkeeper even diving the wrong way may be able to get a leg or hand to block the ball.

GOALKEEPING

The goalkeeper is a team's final line of defence. Much of the time, the outfield players will defend an opposition attack successfully. But when the defence is breached, the goalkeeper is expected to be ready and in position to save their side. Top goalkeepers are applauded for their amazing agility as they spring high in the air or make a spectacular diving save. But much of a top keeper's game is about positioning and awareness to stop shots, and cut out crosses and through-balls.

A goalkeeper has a massive responsibility to their team and should stay alert throughout a match. This, along with good positioning, can frequently see a goalkeeper turn what looks like a real threat into an ordinary-looking save. The secret is to watch the ball constantly and get in line with its direction quickly, so that your body presents a second barrier to the ball in case you fumble it.

A goalkeeper's ready position with legs shoulder-width apart, arms in front, head straight and weight on the balls of your feet allows you to move quickly in any direction, such as having to make a quick step to one side to field a bouncing ball.

To gather a ball zipping across the pitch surface, get in line with the ball's direction, drop down onto one knee and use your body as a second safety barrier behind your hands, which scoop up the ball and gather it into your chest.

Goalkeeping Expert: Iker Casillas

Iker Casillas is widely recognized as one of the best goalkeepers in the world, famed for both his agility and quick reactions. His goalkeeping technique allows him to save wide shots that are hard to reach. Many claim he has reached legendary status since captaining the Spanish team in the 2010 World Cup and leading them to glory. At that moment, Casillas became the third ever goalkeeper to captain a winning team at a World Cup. He showed perfect timing, saving shots from two one-on-one situations. Casillas's consistent goalkeeping skills also saw him earn the Golden Glove, the World Cup's best goalkeeper award.

Did you know?

England's Joe Hart is regarded as one of the best young goalkeepers in the world. The Euro 2012 Qualifier match against Bulgaria gave him his first competitive cap, where he made three crucial saves.

Diving

However good your positioning and anticipation are, you will be called upon to make some diving saves. Staying on the balls of your feet often allows you to take one or two shuffle steps to the side the ball is flying, before launching off your leg nearest the ball to make a dive. Whether the dive is high to your right or low to your left, get your arms up and out so that you aim to collect the ball in front of you. This allows you to watch the ball right into your hands.

As a goalkeeper you often have the very best view of how the game is progressing, especially when the action is in your half. Make sure you pass on any advice clearly and briefly to team-mates. You are the boss in these situations so make your instructions definite and get defenders where you want them to be, in the same way that top keepers like Gianluigi Buffon and Petr Cech do.

To make a good diving save, spring hard off the foot that is nearest to the ball, extend your arms and watch the ball into your hands, which should be held to make a W shape. When you come back down to earth, try to land on the side of your body, on your hips and shoulders.

If diving at an attacker's feet, make sure you get the ball before touching the player, otherwise the referee may award a penalty.

One-on-Ones

One of the ultimate challenges that any goalkeeper faces is when an attacker bursts through the defence, creating a one-on-one situation. This is when you have to mix bravery and rapid reactions with clear thinking and understanding of your position and your goal. Coming off their goal line, a goalkeeper tries to narrow the angle available to the striker, cutting back the view of the goal and using a wide stance with their arms up to make themselves as big as possible.

If the attacker shoots early, try to get some part of your body on the ball to prevent it heading goalwards. If the attacker pushes the ball too far ahead of them or loses control for a moment, you may be able to dive at their feet, spreading yourself to make a long barrier protecting your goal. Claim the ball with both hands and wrap your body around it.

Catching

Crosses into the box are often made with plenty of other players around. In these situations, a keeper needs to be decisive, strong and react quickly. You need to follow the flight of the ball and, if the cross is high, time your spring upwards to meet the ball at the highest point of your jump, with your arms out above and slightly ahead of you to catch the ball cleanly with two hands.

When you sense you cannot gather the ball cleanly, consider making a punch. Make your hands into fists, and thrust your arms and fists forward through the ball in order to send the ball up and away out of danger. Keep your wrists firm as you strike and, as soon as it's done, get back into position. If you can't punch it away, try to deflect it some other way. Top keepers look to deflect the ball with the open palm of their hand round the goalpost or tip the ball up and over the crossbar.

Goalkeepers work on their flexibility and reactions in training throughout their career. Here, this keeper works on his ability to catch the ball from different positions.

Throwing

How a goalkeeper throws or kicks the ball is called distribution. Don't aimlessly kick the ball up the pitch unless there is no alternative. As soon as the ball is safely under your control, start scanning the pitch for opportunities to throw or pass to a team-mate. Stay aware for any lurking opponents at all times.

Goalkeepers can make one of three types of throw. An underarm throw sees you get low and roll the ball out. It is good for accuracy over short distances.

To make a long-distance overarm throw, swing your arm holding the ball from behind you in a bowling motion, with your arm and ball travelling over your head. Aim your throw accurately, with your arm following through and pointing in the direction you wish the ball to travel.

Kicking

Goalkeepers now need to kick the ball more than ever after the new back-pass rule was brought in. The speed and intensity of the game means that the person between the sticks has to control and distribute the ball quickly and accurately.

As a goalkeeper, it's important to concentrate on getting distance and height on clearances from the ground. Follow through on the ball with power and be sure to make a good connection with your foot.

When kicking out of your hands, distance and height is again important, but so is precision and finding a team-mate or an area of the pitch with a bit of space. Take a good run-up, watch the ball onto your foot after releasing it from your hand, before striking it as hard as you can on the volley. With a drop kick, it is again important to consider how you follow through with your leg.

Drop the ball from around waist height just in front of your standing foot as your leg swings back. Just as the ball reaches the floor, connect with the bottom half of the ball and follow through to send the ball long and high up the pitch.

LAWS OF THE GAME

To keep football a beautiful sport, full of excitement and action, you'll have to know the Laws of the Game. Keeping your focus on the match and respecting your opponents and the referee are all crucial to success.

 ## Common Sense

Many players have lost the game for their team by getting sent off. Being one player down can seriously affect the team's performance in the remainder of the match. It's also important to remember that, in many competitions, a red card can also put you out of future matches.

 ## Respect Officials

It is crucial that all matches are fair and are played safely. Officials are an authority on the pitch and their decisions should be respected at all times.

 ## Respect Your Opponents

You'll want to beat your opponents on the pitch, but victory won't feel right unless it's been achieved fairly. All players should want to play a fair game, and you never know, your opponents could one day become team-mates.

 ## Respect Yourself

Football matches are extremely demanding, both physically and mentally. To be at your best, you have to warm up and stretch properly, as well as attend every training session. Make sure you eat a healthy diet and sleep well.

GLOSSARY

Backheel   Using the back of your boot to strike the ball behind you.

Bending   Striking the ball off-centre so that it curves in the air.

Block tackle   Where a player, facing their opponent, strikes the middle of the ball using the inside of the tackling foot.

Chipping   A stabbing-down movement of your foot behind the ball to make it rise into the air, then land sharply.

Control   Your ability to keep control of the ball with your feet, or head, in a match situation.

Cushioning   Slowing down the pace of the ball by relaxing the part of the body receiving it and moving backwards.

Dragback   A popular dribbling trick where you use the sole of your foot to drag the ball backwards as you pivot on your other foot. It is used to beat an opponent. A double dragback is where the same move is done twice in quick succession.

Dribbling   Controlling the football closely with your feet whilst running.

Drive   Striking the ball with instep when making long-range passing shots or powerful kicks when shooting.

Feint   A movement of the body where a player pretends to carry out an action, but then does another in order to fool an opponent.

Flicking   Striking the ball with a brief, accurate touch so that it reaches its target.

Heading   Striking the ball with your head, either to pass to a team-mate or attempt a goal.

Instep   The laced area across the top of your boots, allowing for powerful and long-distance passes or strikes.

Inswinger	A cross or corner that curls towards the goal.
Jockeying	A defensive technique which delays your opponent's progress on the ball, without making a tackle.
Marking	A key defensive ploy, staying close to your opposing players to prevent them gaining control of the ball and potentially scoring.
Nutmeg	A move where you can pass the ball through the defender's legs and collect the ball the other side.
Outswinger	A cross or corner that curls away from the goal.
Push pass	Striking the ball with the side of the foot over short distances.
Set piece	A way of restarting the game in a dead-ball situation. Common set pieces are free kicks, corners, throw-ins and penalties.
Shielding	Using your body as a shield between the ball and your opponent as you keep control of the ball.
Sidefoot	The inside length of your kicking foot. The most accurate method to strike the ball and a commonly used technique in passing.
Stepover	A common feinting move to use whilst dribbling. You feint to play the ball in one direction, then push the ball in the other direction to swerve past your opponent.
Through-ball	A pass behind the other team's defence, requiring good timing and weighting of the ball.
Volley	Striking the ball with the foot when it is in the air.
Warm-down	A post-match routine to relax the body and prevent muscles from stiffening.
Warm-up	A training and pre-match routine to prepare your muscles for physical activity.

INDEX